Laura Krokos

Discover God's Calling for Your Life

A Workbook

ISBN 978-1518872013

To order additional copies of this resource, order online at www.MissionalWomen.com

Printed in the United States of America.

Contents

The Author

 Laura is married and has five kids, two of whom are adopted and another on the way. Laura and her husband have been missionaries to college students for fourteen years where she serves as the Women's Development Coordinator with Master Plan Ministries. She has discipled over two hundred women, led over forty Bible studies and speaks to college and women's groups. Laura is the Founder of the internationally popular blog MissionalWomen.com and has authored five books, including an award winning twelve week Bible Study on First Samuel, *Beholding Him, Becoming Missional, Reach; How to Use Your Social Media Influence for the Glory of God*, and *A Devotional Journey through Judges.*

Introduction

If we go through life without a clearly defined calling then we will be subject to wondering and confusion on if we are doing what the Lord really desires of us. It will lead to frustration and discouragement and even living a wasted life. Therefore I am grateful you have taken time to reflect and work through this workbook to discover God's calling for your life. I am convinced that knowing your calling will help you live a confident, effective life that pleases the Lord.

The content and questions in this workbook has helped me come to know what God desires of my life and I'm confident He will lead you the same way. But just as anything in this life that produces eternal significance and reward, we can't do it by our own effort and strength alone. It is only when we yield to the Lord's ability by recognizing we need Him and surrendering control that we get to see Him do eternal things through our minds, hearts and actions. Take a moment to ask God if there is any unconfessed sin to restore your friendship/fellowship with Him. Then yield control of your life and ask Him to lead you by His Spirit.

My prayer is that at the end of this workbook you will have a clearly defined calling by which to measure all your activity in this life and practical goals to help walk out the calling the Lord has for you.

Praying for you,

Laura

Ideas of How to Use This Workbook

There are many ways you can use this workbook. I will give you some ideas but the basic goal is to come away with a clear picture of why you exist and how you practically can live it out.

Each of us has a unique set of life circumstances which will determine the most realistic way to get the most out of this workbook. Here are some ideas, think through which one would work best for you and your season of life.

❖ Work through the workbook individually. You could work through a little each day or do the entire workbook in one day. How fun it would be to have a personal weekend getaway to spend hearing from the Lord.

❖ You could gather some friends and work through the workbook chapter by chapter as a Bible study.

❖ You could organize a weekend getaway/retreat for a group of friends or your women's group or ministry and work through the workbook together or individually on the retreat. This could be a training retreat or it could be a personal connect with the Lord retreat where you come together for meals and sharing what you've been learning and reading in the evenings.

Knowing Your Purpose
Chapter One

If today was the last day of your life, what would you look back and wish about your life and how you spent your life?

Joe Ehrmann, former NFL coach tells of a statistic of people in the twilight of their lives and what they wish they would have done differently. The top three things are, **they wish they would have risked more, reflected more and did more that outlived them.**

Have you ever taken the time to process your life in terms of wasting it or not wasting it? What would it look like to waste it? And what would make your life successful? Is it making money, enjoying your career, being happy, being liked or accomplishing something great? Or maybe it's helping as many people as possible or having a family? What really defines if we waste our life? What can we live for that will help us not come to the end of our life and wish we would have risked more, reflected more and did more to outlive us?

God, the One who built not only our cells but our souls says in Isaiah 43:7 that we are created for His glory. How incredible! We don't have to wonder why we exist or what our purpose is in life, the Creator and Sustainer of life spelled it out for us. Our purpose is to glorify God. Perhaps if you and I were sitting at a coffee shop together and you asked, "What is my purpose?" and God materialized at the table, wrote something on a piece of paper and slid it over to you the full impact would be felt. But instead of a little scratch piece of paper, He wrote it in Isaiah along with an entire book for you. God tells you that He created you with a purpose, a very fulfilling purpose, to glorify Him. So this life we've been given is wasted when we do not live for the glory of God.

But what does glorify mean? Does it mean to sing or praise Him with our words? No, glorify means to behold and reflect; to look at something and display it to others. So to glorify God, means to fix your eyes on Him and show the world what He is like; to know God and make Him known.

I love how John Piper explains it, "God created us to live with a single passion to joyfully display his supreme excellence in all the spheres of life." We are designed and put here on earth during this specific time period to see and display God's character. God tells us that as we truly know Him, we will reflect Him, *"And we all, who with unveiled faces contemplate the Lord's glory, are being transformed into his image with ever-increasing glory, which comes from the Lord, who is the Spirit."* (2 Corinthians 3:18) When we see Him as He truly is, we are changed from the inside out by the work of the Holy Spirit and we begin to reflect Him more and more. We become what we are gazing at.

So what is your purpose in life? You exist to show a lost and dying world what God is like; to make the invisible God visible to a people desperately loved by their Creator.

Write Out a Prayer:

Process how you feel and think about how God has told you what your purpose is; to know Him and make Him known. How is this different than what you have previously thought?

Read Daniel 11:32

"...But the people who know their God will display strength and take action."

❖ What stands out to you about this verse?

❖ How have you seen this lived out in someone's life?

Knowing truth about God is perhaps the most defining thing about us. It's been said that the most important thing about us is what we believe about God. Everything we think, say, do and feel can come back to something we believe about God, whether true or false.

Try It Out

- ❖ What is something you said or did recently?

- ❖ What does that action show you that you believe about God?

- ❖ What does Scripture say is true about God?

- ❖ How would the action been different if you truly believed the above truth about God?

Knowing what's true about God is a huge deal. We obviously, being finite, can never know all there is to know about God, but He is gracious enough to reveal Himself in part to us in a way we can understand. Romans 1:20 tells us that He has been revealing His character from the beginning of time, *"From the creation of the world His invisible attributes, that is, His eternal power and divine nature, have been clearly seen, being understood through what He has made."* We can get to know God most easily through His Word and the life of Christ (*"For in Him the entire fullness of God's nature dwells bodily."* Colossians 2:9) but His character like His power and nature can also be seen through what He's created.

For instance, let's take the earth, in order to even be able to live on our planet there has to be at least twenty things true of our planet. Here are just a few:

- We need to have a large moon ¼ the size of earth so the gravitational pull stabilizes the angle of our axes, keeping our seasons straight.
- The earth has to have just the right thickness of crust; 4-30 miles thick to regulate the earth's interior temperature.
- We have to be in the exact right place from the sun; the galactic habitable zone. If we were too close to the sun, it is too hot and our oceans would boil, if we were further away it would be too cold and our oceans would freeze. The habitable zone is relatively narrow, if we were 5% closer to sun, it would cause temperatures of 900%.
- There needs to be movement of liquid iron generating the magnetic field.
- The type of star we rotate around has to be a G2 main sequence dwarf star. If it were smaller, the habitable zone would be smaller and we would have to be closer which would knock our rotation into synchronization with the sun and only ½ of the earth would get sun.
- The atmosphere has to have the perfect ratio of nitrogen and oxygen. 78% nitrogen, 21%oxygen, 1%carbon dioxide which ensures protection from sun.
- The earth has to have liquid water.
- It has to be protected by gas giant planets.
- It has to have a nearly circular orbit.
- Needs to have the correct mass.

- It has to have a magnetic field.
- It needs to have plate tectonics.
- It needs the correct ratio of liquid water and continents.

The probability of all these things coming together in one location at the same time is 1 in one thousand trillion, or 1 one thousandth of one one trillionth,

$$\frac{1}{1,000,000,000,000,000}.$$

So the fact that we are alive on this planet gives us a glimpse of the massive knowledge and wisdom of God. *"Then the LORD answered Job out of the storm. He said: "Who is this that darkens my counsel with words without knowledge? Brace yourself like a man; I will question you, and you shall answer me. "Where were you when I laid the earth's foundation? Tell me, if you understand. Who marked off its dimensions? Surely you know! Who stretched a measuring line across it? On what were its footings set, or who laid its cornerstone-- while the morning stars sang together and all the angels shouted for joy?"* Job 38:1-7 **God is a master Designer** and is **more intelligent than we are capable of grasping** even a tiny speck of.

But get this, when God made solar eclipses He revealed something incredible about Himself. In a solar eclipse, the moon blocks the sun from the earth. In order for solar eclipses to be a solar eclipse, the sun has to be four hundred times bigger than the moon and exactly four hundred times further away. (Or a different number with that exact ratio) A solar eclipse allows astronomers to measure atmosphere and allows for discovery of the chromosphere. If the moon were even a sliver smaller it would allow for too much light and therefore scientist couldn't see the light spectrum. If the moon was even slightly bigger it would block part of the atmosphere so this perfect proportion allows for astronomers to understand how the stars work and also for scientists to learn about light.

Ok, how crazy, that this event in creation, the radiance of the sun is blocked just enough for us to get a glimpse of light. This shouts Exodus 34 to me. Moses calls out, Lord show me your glory, let me see You, let me know You. Let me see your extra-spectacularness, let me see the S on your chest. And guess what God does? He answered Moses' request, but has to block His radiance in order for Moses to be able to see and understand His incredibleness. He gave Moses a glimpse of His glory; His patience, grace and justice. Solar eclipses show us that God makes a way for us to know Him. He brings together all the right circumstances for us to be able to get a glimpse of what He is really like, just as the sun's radiance is blocked making way for us to understand light. **God wants to be known.**

Ok and get this, the very best place to view solar eclipse is from the earth, not anywhere else in our solar system. So the one place that has observers is the one place that has the best eclipses. God created a place for us to be able to discover. He knows the satisfaction it would bring for us to learn and discover and be in awe of His creation.

So not only does God want to be known, He created this universe in the most pleasurable way for us, in a way for us to find deep satisfaction in discovery and delight in Him as the Creator.

So in learning about the earth's habitability, we see that God is an Intelligent Designer. Through solar eclipses we see that God wants to be known and is capable of helping us see and known Him. But these are just two characteristics of God out of an innumerable amount since God is eternal and everything about Him is eternal.

Let me share just one more, the wild tobacco plant. The wild tobacco plant seed needs wildfire to germinate and grow. Once it germinates it grows and has to be ready for anything because every part of it is attacked by a specialist that feeds on a particular part of the plant.

But the wild tobacco is ready. It has a secret chemical weapon. When an herbivore attacks, it ramps up a toxin called nicotine. The nicotine poisons anything that has a muscle. So, now our little plant has survived, not being eaten by bugs. However here

13

comes Mr. Caterpillar who has no muscles. This secret chemical weapon doesn't work on him. Now our little plant is being eaten alive and chances are if nothing happens the entire plant will be devoured in a couple days by Mr. chubby Caterpillar.

But as we know all wild tobacco plants haven't all been eaten alive. Are you curious why? It's because it has yet another secret weapon. When Mr. Caterpillar's saliva gets on the leaves the plants releases an odor which is picked up by the very bugs that eat caterpillars. Basically the plant sends out secret SOS smells and calls in reinforcements. Within hours Mr. Caterpillar Eating Bug comes along and gobbles up Mr. Caterpillar.

And if that weren't enough, the plant also makes little lollipop looking things called a tricomb. The caterpillar eats these yummy little treats and twenty minutes later the secret weapon kicks in and Mr. Caterpillar himself now emits a very appetizing smell to Mr. Bug. Pretty amazing right. But there's even more secret weapons!

Here comes Mrs. Hawk Moth gathering nectar from the flower of the plant. But moths also lay up to two hundred eggs which grow into tobacco eating caterpillars. So if little tobacco plant happens to get too many little Hawk Moth eggs on it, it changes the shape of its flower from short and open to tall and narrow. Now Mrs. Hawk Moth can't get the pollen and along comes Mrs. Hummingbird whose beak fits perfectly inside the long flower.

This little wildflower of the field has at least three defense mechanisms tailor fit for its different predators.

So I hope you're wondering how in the world this relates shows us God's character because now we getting to the fun part!

Before the fall of mankind in the garden these little plants didn't need any of these amazing mechanisms. There was no blood shed and animals didn't eat each other. But here we have a plant without a brain that has defense mechanisms. So why would God give this little flower so many defense mechanisms if it had no need to defend itself?

The fall didn't surprise or catch God off guard. And it wasn't His plan B. God knew what would happen and provided for Mr. Wild Tobacco Flower long before he ever even existed. Perhaps the tobacco plant could have wondered why it needed an odor releasing mechanism. Perhaps it felt stifled with a part of it going unused.

The flowers of the field show us that God knows what is needed long before we ever see the need and He provides. Just like long before the wild tobacco plant needed to have a way to ward off enemies, He provided. Long ago He knew what you needed and set out to provide for you, to act on your behalf. And provide abundantly.

The wildflowers show us sin and brokenness hasn't hindered God's plan for your life. He cares enough to help a plant fight against a caterpillar, sure He cares much more for you, a valuable being created in His image.

"Learn how the wildflowers of the field grow: they don't labor or spin thread. Yet I tell you that not even Solomon in all his splendor was adorned like one of these! (Could you imagine Solomon's soldiers having releasing odors chemical weapons). *If that's how God clothes the grass of the field, which is here today and thrown into the furnace tomorrow, won't He do much more for you-you of little faith? So don't worry, saying, 'What will we eat?' or 'What will we drink?' or 'What will we wear?' For the idolaters eagerly seek all these things, and your heavenly Father knows that you need them. But seek first the kingdom of God and His righteousness, and all these things will be provided for you."* Matthew 6:28-33 {Parenthesis mine}

The wildflowers of the field show us God is a much better provider than we ever give Him credit for.

15

God Sightings

The Lord desires for us to see Him and know Him and giving us multiple opportunities every day.

❖ How has God been revealing Himself to you? Think about your last couple days. What can you see about God's character from your interactions, activities, relationships or observations?

Awe of God Exercise

God is infinite; without end or limit. So to really get a bigger grasp on this, write down as many characteristics of God you can think of. Try to find a verse that demonstrates that attribute of God. You may need to use a concordance.

We could spend our entire life and all of eternity writing down characteristics about God and would still never come to the end of knowing all there is to know about Him. But not only is He unending in good characteristics, each of the characteristics themselves. Each attribute of God we learn about is also inexhaustible, unending, unlimited. For instance, we will never come to the end of His love or intelligence.

Pick one characteristic you wrote down above and fill it in the blanks below.

His _____ is never-ending. We will never come to the end of God's _____ no matter how much we fail. We will never be able to fully measure the depths of God's _____. His _____ is inexhaustible. His _____ is unlimited. He will never run out of _____.

The people God uses greatly, the ones who are the most fulfilled are the ones who have an intimate, passionate relationship with Him, which comes from saturating themselves in the Word of God. The more we know God, the more we want to make Him known. And the best way to get to know God deeply is by spending time with Him in His Word.

The more we know the truth about what God is like, the more our actions will reflect what God is like. Therefore the best use of our time could be growing in our knowledge of God.

- ❖ What could it look like in your daily life to have time set aside to grow in the knowledge of God?

Our purpose is to glorify God, to know Him and therefore reflect Him. Let's move onto how that is worked out into our everyday life.

Reliance on the Lord
Chapter Two

The Lord in John chapter 15 tells us we can do nothing of eternal significance apart from Him. *"Just as a branch is unable to produce fruit by itself unless it remains on the vine, so neither can you unless you remain in Me. "I am the vine; you are the branches. The one who remains in Me and I in him produces much fruit, because you can do nothing without Me."* John 15:4-5

Glorifying God; knowing Him and making Him known and living out our calling is impossible. Yet with God all things are possible. When we yield to Him and let Him live His life through us, then we can live out the eternal purpose and mission He has for us in a balanced way. Practically what that means is admitting to the Lord we need Him and surrendering the control to Him the minute we realize we have sinned or chosen to live unreliant on Him. (To see a diagram explaining more fully what this practically looks like go to www.MissionalWomen.com/videos)

Read Galatians 3:3 and 5:16-17

"Are you so foolish? After beginning with the Spirit, are you now going to be made complete by the flesh?" (3:3), "I say then, walk by the Spirit and you will not carry out the desire of the flesh. For the flesh desires what is against the Spirit, and the Spirit desires what is against the flesh; these are opposed to each other, so that you don't do what you want." (5:16-17)

❖ What does Galatians 3:3 and 5:16-17 say about living the Christian's life in our own strength?

Spiritual breathing is a powerful word picture (developed by Bill Bright) that can help you experience moment-by-moment dependence on the Holy Spirit. Just as there are two parts of breathing, exhaling and inhaling, which help us live, there are two parts to living the spirit-filled life.

We can compare exhaling to confessing, agreeing with God concerning our sin. Confession requires repentance - a change in attitude and action.

The second part can be compared to inhaling, surrendering control of your life to Christ, and relying upon the Holy Spirit to fill you with His presence and power by faith.

This breathing metaphor, called getting Christ on the throne, is a very simple concept; confess and surrender. You don't earn Christ on the throne by having a quiet time or doing other Christian things. It's simply a heart condition of saying no to our flesh and yielding to the Lord. It's much like a little kid asking his dad to tie his shoe, *"I can't, will you"*. Confess and Surrender. We are filled with the Holy Spirit by faith alone and prayer is one way of expressing our faith. The following is a suggested prayer:
Dear Father, I need you. I acknowledge that I have sinned against You by directing my own life. I thank You that You have forgiven my sins through Christ's death on the cross for me. I now invite Christ to again take His place on the throne of my life. Fill me with the Holy Spirit as you commanded me to be filled, and as You promised in Your Word that You would do if I asked in faith. I pray this is the name of Jesus. I now thank you for filling me with the Holy Spirit and directing my life.

Personal Reflection

2 Chronicles 16:9 says, *"For the eyes of the Lord range throughout the earth to strengthen those whole hearts are fully committed to him."*
  ❖ Is your heart fully committed to the Lord? If not, what and why are you withholding from Him?

❖ Are you willing to work and sacrifice your pleasure, resources, time and energy for the sake of God's glory? Why or why not?

❖ Ask God to bring to your mind any unconfessed sin. Spend some time confessing it and surrendering the control of your life to Him. (Remember that if you have put your faith in Christ and His work on the cross to forgive you of your sin, then He forgave all your sin, past present and future. Therefore you confess your sin to restore your fellowship, or friendship with God just as you would with a friend or family member, not to get more forgiveness.) Use the space below to write out a prayer to God.

The Life Direction Circles

Chapter Three

I am a diagram person. I enjoy how a simple drawing can help illustrate something so well. Therefore I designed a diagram to bring understanding in the complexities of how our purpose, mission, current reality and uniqueness fit together. It's called the Life Direction Circles.

Purpose answers the question, "Why do we exist?" Mission answers the question, "What are we here to do?", Our uniqueness is summed up by the characteristics, gifts and values given to us by God and our current reality is the places we spend our time.

To see this diagram explained go to www.MissionalWomen.com/Videos The video is titled, "*How to Live on Purpose for the Glory of God.*"

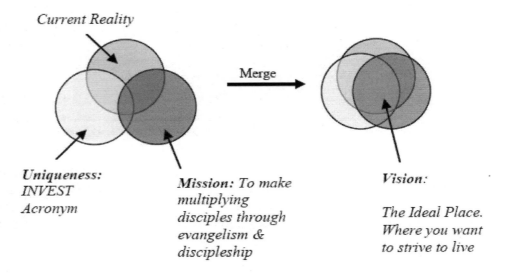

Purpose: To glorify God.
To know God and make Him known.

Current Reality

Merge

Uniqueness:
INVEST
Acronym

Mission: To make
multiplying
disciples through
evangelism &
discipleship

Vision:

The Ideal Place.
Where you want
to strive to live

We've talked about our purpose being to glorify God; to know Him and make Him known. Every person has the same purpose in life. God has also given every believer a specific mission called the Great Commission; the mission of making multiplying disciples through the process of evangelism and discipleship. All believers have the same purpose and the same mission yet are all created very differently. Your uniqueness, how God built you, and your current reality also play a role in your specific calling.

The tendency is to focus on one circle at a time like trying to live out your strengths or enjoying your current season of life. But living for just one of these circles leads to frustration and ineffectiveness in your calling.

The goal is to merge these together as much as possible. Let's use Jesus as our example of how to merge these. He used His uniqueness of being able to heal (so people would know He was God) to preach the Gospel. His current reality was traveling around to preach the Gospel. In Mark 1:29-33 we see His uniqueness was getting a little more attention as people were coming to Him to heal their friends and family but weren't as interested in hearing the Gospel message. So in order to live out His calling without leaving out the mission He changed up His current reality. He said in 1:38, *"Come let us go to the towns nearby so I may preach there also, for that is what I came for."* He didn't let the message of the Gospel get pushed aside by His uniqueness of doing good deeds or by His current reality.

The law of entropy says things naturally go from order to disorder. So unless we are intentional about a plan to merge these circles, in all reality it won't happen. In the following chapters our mission, uniqueness and current reality will be defined and you'll get a picture of what it looks like for you to merge your circles. Let's start with current reality.

Defining Your Current Reality
Chapter Four

No two people have the same exact current reality. Your current reality is the specific places you spend your time. It's your unique sphere of influence. These places are the spaces God wants you to live out your purpose and mission. So let's define what sphere of influence, or current reality He has placed you in.

Each of us is given the same 168 hours a week. 56 of those hours on average are spent sleeping. Fill out the chart below with your weekly activities to find where you spend the rest of your time. Include meals and every other use of your time.

Under the Time column write in when you get up and fill in the times by hour till you go to bed. Then fill in each activity in the correct box. Then fill in extra things like make dinner, grocery shop, laundry etc.

"Teach us to number our days carefully so that we may develop wisdom in our hearts."
Psalm 90:12

Time	M	T	W	Th	F	S	S

25

❖ Looking at the chart, where is the majority of your time spent? What are the second and third largest chunks of time spent?

   1.

   2.

   3.

❖ Where are you mentally and emotionally most connected?

❖ Which is the most life-giving? Most draining?

❖ What stands out to you about seeing your current reality on paper?

❖ Spend some time talking to God about where you spend your time and adjustments you'd like to make.

Uncovering the Mission
Chapter Five

Read and write down what Jesus' mission was in your own words.

John 3:16-17

"For God loved the world in this way: He gave His One and Only Son, so that everyone who believes in Him will not perish but have eternal life. For God did not send His Son into the world that He might condemn the world, but that the world might be saved through Him."

John 12:44-46

"Then Jesus cried out, "The one who believes in Me believes not in Me, but in Him who sent Me. And the one who sees Me sees Him who sent Me. I have come as a light into the world, so that everyone who believes in Me would not remain in darkness."

John 17:24

"Father, I desire those You have given Me to be with Me where I am. Then they will see My glory, which You have given Me because You loved Me before the world's foundation."

John 20:19-21

In the evening of that first day of the week, the disciples were [gathered together] with the doors locked because of their fear of the Jews. Then Jesus came, stood among them, and said to them, "Peace to you!" Having said this, He showed them His hands and His side. So the disciples rejoiced when they saw the Lord. Jesus said to them again, "Peace to you! As the Father has sent Me, I also send you."

John 20:30-31

"Jesus performed many other signs in the presence of His disciples that are not written in this book. But these are written so that you may believe Jesus is the Messiah, the Son of God, and by believing you may have life in His name."

Luke 5:32

"I have not come to call the righteous, but sinners to repentance."

Luke 19:10

"For the Son of Man has come to seek and to save the lost."

Read and write down the mission Jesus gave believers in your own words.

John 20:21

Jesus said to them again, "Peace to you! As the Father has sent Me, I also send you."

Matthew 28:18-20

"Then Jesus came near and said to them, "All authority has been given to Me in heaven and on earth. Go, therefore, and make disciples of all nations, baptizing them in the name of the Father and of the Son and of the Holy Spirit, teaching them to observe everything I have commanded you. And remember, I am with you always, to the end of the age."

Summarize all these verses into a paragraph describing what Jesus sent us to do.

Jesus' mission was to bring salvation so people would see the Father as He truly is. This is the mission He gives to all who receive that salvation. The strategy is make multiplying disciples through evangelism and discipleship.

Evangelism

God is at work in the lives of people around us, but it seems so often that our fears keep us from even getting into conversations with them to find out. Bill Bright, the founder of Campus Crusade says "Successful witnessing is taking initiative to share Christ in the power of the Holy Spirit and leaving the results up to Him." And really that is all we can do. God is the one that changes hearts, but He has called us to be part of the adventure of telling them His story.

For ten years I did not share my faith. I would invite my friends to church and youth group hoping someone else would share the actual gospel with them. Ten years is a long time to not be obedient to what God calls us to do. And like Romans 1 talks about, when we disobey God, our hearts become hardened. This is what happened to me.

I went to college wanting to be involved in ministry. I liked the idea of girls coming to know Jesus and I wanted to be the one that would help them grow into strong disciples after they had given their lives to Him. But whenever the topic of evangelism would come up, I had a very arrogant attitude and would get angry at anyone who disagreed with me. I distorted the verse, *"Always be prepared to give an answer to everyone who asks you to give the reason for the hope that you have."* (1 Pet. 3:15) and made that to mean that you don't go to people, you let them come to you. As a result I would get very angry at people who were taking initiative to share the Gospel. I honestly thought, *"They are just making my job harder because now the non-believer is offended and I have to befriend them and win them back."* When I think about this, I am embarrassed of my self-centeredness and sad about all the opportunities wasted because of my arrogance. But praise God that He is able to soften even the hardest of hearts.

I hope you are wondering what happened. How did God change my hard heart? Well, God blessed me with Austin. We met after I had returned from a missions trip and we hit it off. Austin and I were both student leaders for Master Plan Ministries in Durango Colorado. Austin and our friend John were constantly sharing their faith. At first it bothered me thinking they were offending people. But rather than seeing people offended by them sharing the Gospel with them, they were seeing fruit of people surrendering their lives to Christ. I couldn't believe it! When I looked back on my Christian life, not one person had ever come up to me and asked me to share the Gospel with them. Who knew? Sure, there were people that came to Christ because I invited them somewhere, but it was not because I took the initiative to start the conversation with them. And it never seemed like I was good enough friends to share the Gospel with them. And when I finally did become good enough friends it was awkward that I hadn't talked about the most important thing in my life. So one day I said to Austin, *"Ok, walk through with me what you say to people when you share the Gospel."* I was going to see if it would be something I would get offended at if I were a non-believer. God used that conversation to change my heart and attitude for life. Austin used the Four Spiritual Laws developed by Bill Bright in a conversational way. He was not cramming anything, it wasn't a canned presentation, just a simple conversation. I thought, *"I can do this,"* So I tried it out. It felt totally normal (once I could get enough guts up to get into a spiritual conversation) and God blessed me with being able to see eternal fruit born for His kingdom by girls surrendering their life to Christ because of our conversation.

I am not sure where your heart attitude is with sharing your faith, but I am pretty sure that you are probably not as hard hearted about it as I was. And even if you are, will you be willing to let God shape your opinions about it today?

There are many aspects of the Great Mission God has given us so too help us talk through them, let's use a MAP. M.A.P. stands for Methods, Avenues, and Point.

Methods

There are numerous means available to communicate the unchanging Gospel message. Some tools are better fit for different situations. So it's best to have a well-supplied toolbox to pull out what is needed when you need it. I recommend working with one tool until you are completely confident with it and then move on to another.

Some methods of sharing the Gospel:

Biblical presentations

- ❖ Romans Road (Reading Romans 3:23, 6:23, 5:8, 10:9-10)
- ❖ Would You Like to Know God Personally? booklet. {Order at CampusCrusade.com}
- ❖ The Bridge illustration {Training to draw it at http://www.evangelismcoach.org/2008/how-to-use-the-bridge-illustration or order booklet at http://www.navpress.com}
- ❖ Ray Comfort's Way of the Master Questions {WayoftheMaster.com}

Testimonial presentations

- ❖ The story of how you came to see your need for forgiveness and surrender your life to Christ. {Worksheet to help you write it out at MissionalWomen.com}
- ❖ Stories of how God came through for you and how you better saw His character.

Philosophical arguments

- ❖ Apologetics {Why we believe what we believe. Resources at GotQuestions.org}
- ❖ Who is Jesus Bible study {Ordered at CruStore.org/who-is-this-jesus-mini-magazine}
- ❖ Trilema {Explanation found at Greatcom.org/resources/areadydefense/ch21/default}

But in order to use these tools, you have to break four Sound Barriers developed by Campus Crusade.

Sound Barriers

1. Getting into a simple conversation. What's your name, how are you etc..
2. Swinging the conversation to spiritual things.
3. Sharing the Gospel.
4. Asking them to respond to the Gospel by asking for a decision.

- ❖ Which barrier is hardest for you to get through in conversations?

Questions are a great tool to help you break through each sound barrier. Here are a couple of examples.

Do you have any kind of spiritual beliefs?

If you died right now and were standing before God and He said, "Why should I let you into heaven" What would you say?

If what you were believing is not true, would you want to know?

❖ Which question above (or a question of your own) are you most comfortable asking to help you break through each sound barrier?

Avenues

As God works through believers to seek and save the lost, there are three different types of relational avenues which give us opportunity to use our tools. These avenues are determined by the nature of the relationship between the believer and the unbeliever.

1. Organic: Getting into conversations with others in the normal course of life. Read the verses below and write down how it is an example of this mode. John 1:40-51

John 4:1-42

Colossians 4:5-6

1 Peter 3:15

- ❖ Describe a modern day example of this avenue.

- ❖ What are some pro's and con's of this avenue?

2. Community: Inviting non-believers to be part of your believing community. Letting them see how believers interact and using this to get into a spiritual conversation with them.

Read the examples below and write down a few key words or a sentence reminding you what it says.

John 17:21-23

John 13:34-35

Acts 2:42-47

- ❖ Describe a modern day example.

- ❖ What are some pro's and con's of this avenue?

3. Missional: Intentionally taking the Gospel to an individual you have not met.

Read the examples below and write down a few key words or a sentence reminding you what it says.

2 Timothy 4:2

Mark 1:38-39

Luke 9:1-6, 10:1-17

Acts 8

Acts 11:19-24

❖ Describe a modern day example.

❖ What are some pro's and con's of this avenue?

❖ Through which of these avenues did you come to Christ?

❖ Which of these does your believing community emphasizes?

❖ Which one of these avenues is the most challenging for you personally? Why?

❖ Are all three of these avenues necessary to saturate our culture with the Gospel? Why?

Point

The point of the Gospel is the message of how we are saved. If we get this wrong, we totally miss it. So, what is the Gospel message? What things does someone have to understand to be transferred from the kingdom of darkness to the kingdom of light?

❖ What does Colossians 1:21-23 say the Gospel is? What key points does someone need to understand the full Gospel?

❖ What would be the result if someone trying to understand the Gospel did not understand each of the following truths?
Romans 3:23

Romans 6:23

Romans 5:8

Romans 10:9-10,13

Philemon 6 says, *"I pray that you may be active in sharing your faith, so that you will have a full understanding of every good thing we have in Christ."* When we share our faith we get to experience God and see His mighty hand working in people's lives.

Matthew 9:37 says, the harvest is plentiful, but the people willing to share the Gospel are few. John 12:32-33 tells us God is already working on every person in your sphere of influence. And Acts 17:26 says, *"From one man he made every nation of men, that they should inhabit the whole earth; and he determined the times set for them and the exact places where they should live."* You have been placed strategically in this very place, for this very time!

Discipleship

The Great Co-Mission God has given us has two parts, evangelism and discipleship. Now that we've covered the basics of evangelism, let's talk about discipleship.

Discipleship is helping someone become stronger in their relationship with God. I like long time missionary Roger Hershey's definition, "Helping someone walk by faith, communicate their faith and multiply their faith." So the main goal of discipling someone is helping them become able to have a strong relationship with God on their own, share the Gospel, disciple others and teach others to do the same.

Again, there is a handy diagram that helps bring clarity to this. You can find the video at MissionalWomen.com/videos titled "How to Live Missionally"

When thinking about discipling someone it's best to keep it simple. Help them grow in their faith which Romans 10 tells us faith comes by hearing the Word of God. So help them get a strong grasp of the basics. Tools like the Thrive Discipleship Study (found at MissionalWomen.com by searching the search box) are very helpful.

Helping someone communicate their faith and multiply their faith take a bit more intentionality but are incredibly worth it. The questions on the chart on the next page help bring clarity on how.

Great Commission Funnel Diagram

Meet People

Are they able to meet new people? Where are they meeting new people at? How can you help them?

Evangelism

Sound Barriers
1. Normal Conversation
2. Spiritual Conversation
3. Share the Gospel
4. Ask for a Decision

Can they break each of these barriers? Help them come up with a couple questions to break each sound barrier. Let them see you break the barriers and give them opportunity.

Can they train someone in these things?

Discipleship

Are they familiar with the basics of the faith (thrive study)? Do they know how to initiate discipling someone else? Have you shown them the Great Commission funnel & do they have an understanding of multiplication?

42

Believe it or not, reaching this world is very possible. Starting with 45 of us, multiplying once annually the whole world could be reached in 29 years. Here's how Walter Henrichsen explains it. "Let's say for example that a gifted evangelist is able to lead 1,000 people to Christ every day. Each year he will have reached 365,000 people, a phenomenal ministry indeed. Let's compare him with a disciple who leads not 1,000 people a day to Christ, but only one person a year. At the end of the year, the disciple has one convert; the evangelist, 365,000. But suppose the disciple has not only led this man to Christ, but has also discipled him. He has prayed with him, taught him how to feed himself from the Word of God, gotten him into fellowship with like-minded believers, taken him out on evangelism and showed him how to present the Gospel to other people. At the end of that first year, this new convert is able to lead another man to Christ and follow him up as he himself has been followed up.

At the start of the second year, the disciple has doubled his ministry—the one has become two. During the second year, each man goes out and leads not 1,000 people per day to Christ, but one person per year. At the end of the second year, we have four people. You can see how slow our process is. But note, too, that we do not have only converts, but disciples who are able to reproduce themselves. At this rate of doubling every year, the disciple leading one man per year to Christ, will overtake the evangelist numerically somewhere in the 19th year. From then on, the disciple and his multiplying ministry will be propagating faster than the combined ministry of dozens of gifted evangelists."

Today Jesus is asking you to do something much tougher than dying for Him. He is asking you to live for Him and to make an unreserved commitment of all that you are to Christ and His mission of evangelism and discipleship on earth.

We are only on this earth for a short time. God describes the nations, all people, throughout all time are like a drop in a bucket. What are you going to do with your split second in eternity?

Personal Reflection

Spend some time thinking/praying/journaling about how you'd like to grow in the area of evangelism and discipleship and what some next steps could be.

Finding Your Uniqueness

Chapter Six

Your purpose is to glorify God; to know God and show the world what He is like. Your mission is to make disciples through the process of evangelism and discipleship and hopefully you now have a clear picture of your current reality and spheres of influence. There is one last piece to the puzzle before we start to make a more practical plan, your uniqueness.

You are beautifully unique and valuable. Not because of anything you've done, but because of who made you. For instance say I had a $100 bill to give you. But I wadded it up and spit on it. Is it still valuable? Of course! Why? Because of who made it. I can print off a $100 bill but it would be worthless. It's only valuable because the US Mint made it. You have unique value because you are an eternally precious masterpiece. Your worth is not based on what you do but because of who made you. You are an eternal God reflector made in the image of God. Your unique experiences, values, strengths, passions and so on show the world what God is like in a way that no one else can.

It's always helpful to write things down so below are questions to help you clearly define how the Lord made you unique. We will use an acronym I made up to help address many areas of your uniqueness. The acronym is INVEST, Interests, Nature, Vision, Experiences, Spiritual Gifts and Treasure. Let's get to it and discovering how God built you to invest in His kingdom.

Interests-
What (types of things) and who (people group, age group etc.) do you enjoy?

Nature/Personality-
What are some strengths and weaknesses mentally, emotionally and socially?

Vision-
What is something you would do in your lifetime for the glory of God if you knew you would not fail?

What are you passionate about? What would others describe you as passionate about?

What are your desires, hopes and dreams for the future?

What verses motivate you the most?

Experiences-
What do you see going on around you and every time you experience it or think about it, it deeply effects you?

What is happening that you desperately want to see different?

What are we uniquely positioned and equipped to do?

Spiritual Gifts-
What comes natural for you to do?

What do you enjoy doing? What thing(s) really refresh and encourage you after you do them?

What have others noticed you were good at?

What have spiritual gift inventory tests said your spiritual gift(s) were?

What are some things you are confident in doing because of the ability God has given you?

Treasure-
What has God entrusted to you? What resources are you a steward of?

Merging Your Circles

Brainstorm ideas of how to use some of things above to share the Gospel and make disciples or give your life toward the Great Commission.

Brainstorm how you can merge these things with your current season of life.

Write down some ideas of how your mission can tie together with your uniqueness and your current reality.

Defining Your Calling

Write down in 1-2 sentences what your specific calling is (your merged circles). Commit this to memory.

How can you be intentional this week about the mission God gave you of making disciples with your current reality and uniqueness?

Practically, what is your next step?

What things could distract you? How can you guard against them?

Making a Plan
Chapter Seven

Planning comes easy for some and not so much for others. And if the logistics of planning were not difficult enough sometimes we can battle our own thoughts on if the Lord really wants us to plan. After all there are verse like, *"Trust in the Lord with all your heart and lean not on your own understanding..."* (Proverbs 3:5) So in order to give our whole heart to making a plan and setting goals, let's go to God's Word and see what He says about planning.

Psalm 20:4 *"He will give you your heart's desire and carry out all your plans."*
As we delight ourselves in the Lord, he will make our desires line up with His (Ps. 37:4) But in order for Him to carry out our plans, there has to be a plan in the first place. And as we make effort to walk it out relying on Him each step, He will redirect us as needed. Just as Psalm 37:5 says, *"Commit your way to the Lord! Trust him! He will act."* The Hebrew word commit is a word picture of rolling a log down a hill. As it bounces around in motion, it can be redirected. You can't move what's not in motion.

Psalm 143:8 *"...Make me know the way I should walk, because I entrust myself to you."*

Proverbs 3:5-6 *"Trust in the LORD with all your heart and lean not on your own understanding; in all your ways acknowledge him, and he will make your paths straight."* This verse is commonly misread as *"lean not on your brain"*. But the Lord created us in His image as great thinkers. But because of the fall, we now think of things apart from Him rather than dependent on Him. Leaning not on our own understanding means to rely and depend on Him as we think. This verse is saying the opposite of what is commonly thought. It is saying to make plans/paths as we trust Him to lead our thinking. Think with Christ on the throne.

Proverbs 4:7 *"Wisdom is supreme; therefore get wisdom. Though it cost all you have, get understanding."* Wisdom is knowledge in action.

Proverbs 14:15 *"A simple man believes anything, but a prudent man gives thought to his steps."*

Proverbs 15:22 *"Plans fail for lack of counsel, but with many advisers they succeed."*

Proverbs 16:3 *"Commit to the LORD whatever you do, and your plans will succeed."*

Proverbs 16:9 *"The heart of man plans his way, but the LORD establishes his steps."* We have a great privilege of partnering with the Lord. As we rely on Him, we get to make plans and depend on Him to make it possible to walk them out.

Proverbs 20:18 *"Make plans by seeking advice..."*

Proverbs 21:5 *"The plans of the diligent lead to profit as surely as haste leads to poverty."*

Isaiah 14:24 *"The LORD Almighty has sworn, "Surely, as I have planned, so it will be, and as I have purposed, so it will stand."* The Lord is a planner and we are built in His image. God is glorified (His character displayed) by planning.

Isaiah 28:28 "All this wisdom comes from the Lord Almighty. The plans God makes are wise, and they always succeed."

Luke 14:28-33 *"Suppose one of you wants to build a tower. Will he not first sit down and estimate the cost to see if he has enough money to complete it? For if he lays the foundation and is not able to finish it, everyone who sees it will ridicule him, saying, 'This fellow began to build and was not able to finish.' "Or suppose a king is about to go to war against another king. Will he not first sit down and consider whether he is able with ten thousand men to oppose the one coming against him with twenty thousand? If he is not able, he will send a delegation while the other is still a long way off and will ask for terms of peace. In the same way, any of you who does not give up everything he has cannot be my disciple."*

John 16:13 *"But when he, the Spirit of truth, comes, he will guide you into all truth."*

Acts 15:22, 28 *"Then the apostles and elders, with the whole church, decided to choose some of their own men and send them to Antioch with Paul and Barnabas. They chose Judas (called Barsabbas) and Silas, two men who were leaders among the brothers...It seemed good to the Holy Spirit and to us not to burden you with anything beyond the following requirements..."*

Romans 2:6 *"For God will reward each of us according to what we have done."* And he who is faithful with little will be entrusted with more. (Matt.25:21)

2 Corinthians 9:6 *"Remember this: The person who plants a little will have a small harvest, but the person who plants a lot will have a big harvest."*

Galatians 6:7-9 *"Don't be deceived: God is not mocked. For whatever a man sows he will also reap, because the one who sows to his flesh will reap corruption from the flesh, but the one who sows to the Spirit will reap eternal life from the Spirit. So we must not get tired of doing good, for we will reap at the proper time if we don't give up.*

Philippians 2:25-26 *"But I considered it necessary to send you Epaphroditus-my brother, co-worker, and fellow soldier, as well as your messenger and minister to my need- since he has been longing for all of you and was distressed because you heard* *that he was sick..."* This is an example of the great apostle Paul planning.

1 Thessalonians 3:1-2 *"Therefore, when we could no longer stand it, we thought it was better to be left alone in Athens. And we sent Timothy, our brother and God's co-worker in the gospel of Christ, to strengthen and encourage you concerning your faith..."* Another example of planning ahead.

It is helpful to remind ourselves of examples from Scripture of people planning. There is Moses in Numbers 13 who though God promised to give the promised land, the Lord also wanted Moses to come up with a plan to walk out. And Joshua in Joshua 6 when they came up with a plan to take over Jericho even though they already knew the Lord would give them the city.

There is also Nehemiah who made extensive long term plans to rebuild the temple walls. And David who made many plans to lead battles and even gathered around him wise men *"Who understood the times and knew what Israel should do"* (1 Chron.12:32).

And even Jesus, God the Creator, planned and prepared. Thinking of Jesus walking on earth like us, He had the disciples go get the donkey to ride on for Passover (wouldn't you just love to know the backstory of that one. Why was the guy so quick to let someone take his donkey?) And even that He was there at Passover to be the Passover Lamb was a plan, fulfilling a prophecy planned a long time before hand, like an eternity beforehand (my mind just exploded in awe of God!) And His entire goal of coming to earth as 100% God and 100% human to seek and save the lost. A plan where He let nothing distract Him.

To plan is wise. And right goals follow wise planning. But we can do nothing truly significant apart from the Lord so we need to yield and let Him have His way in our thinking. We need to do a throne check. As we are yielded/surrendered to the Lord, He does this super awesome thing, He leads our thinking, He illuminates our mind and aligns our thinking with His. (Though there is always a need to bring every thought back to Scripture and make sure it lines up.) The God of the universe helps us understand His will. He the Shepherd helps His sheep to hear His voice. (John 10:27)

Personal Reflection

Spend some time thinking and praying about your thoughts, fears and hesitations about planning. Ask God to help you get to the place of trusting Him more.

Discerning God's Will

Chapter Eight

There can be so much worry involved in knowing God's will. *What if I'm wrong? What if I missed it?* We either blame ourselves or blame God and both scenarios expose a small view of God. But God doesn't want His desires to be a secret. He wants us to know what's best and that is why He gives us a lamp to our feet and tells us to ask for wisdom. So practically how does God reveal His desires, His will to us?

Prerequisite to Knowing God's Will

Romans 12:1-3 talks about giving ourselves entirely to the Lord. Having our minds *(thoughts, hopes, dreams, and aspirations)* transformed by Christ. Then we will know and be an example of what God's will is. So before knowing God's will you need to do a throne check.

As we seek God's will with Christ on the throne of our life, we need to actually ask Him for wisdom. (Wisdom is the right application of knowledge.) And as you can probably tell I like acronyms as much as I like diagrams. So here is an acronym I came up with to help give the fuel or confidence to walk out what God has for you. It is the GAS acronym which stands for God's Word, Ask Mature Believers and Spirit-Filled Reasoning.

God's Word- God's written Word is our ultimate source of authority in all areas of life. What decisions has God already given us clear direction based on the Bible? Ask God to lead you to specific passages of how you fit into His plan.

Ask Mature Believers- Ask for advice from mature Christians who are viewed by many as mature, who are informed about what God is doing around the world, someone who knows you well, someone who will be objective with you and someone who knows and walks with God and knows His ways.

Prov. 11:14 *"For lack of guidance a nation falls, but many advisers make victory sure."*
Prov. 15:22 *"Plans fail for lack of counsel, but with many advisers they succeed."*
Prov. 15:31-33 *"He who listens to a life-giving rebuke will be at home among the wise. He who ignores discipline despises himself, but whoever heeds correction gains understanding. The fear of the LORD teaches a man wisdom, and humility comes before honor."*
Prov. 12:15 *"The way of a fool seems right to him, but a wise man listens to advice."*

Spirit-filled Reasoning- With Christ on the throne think strategic. God has given us a sound and sanctified mind He expects us to love Him with and be a good steward using. And using wisdom and reason will follow the examples of the apostles:
1 Thes. 3:1-2 *"we thought it best..."*
Phil. 2:25, 26 *"I thought it was necessary..."*
1 Cor. 16:3-4 *"if it is fitting..."*
Acts 6:2-4 *"it is not desirable..."*
Acts 15:22, 28 *"it seemed good..."*

Using spirit-filled reasoning usually means asking questions:
How does it fit in the overall plan of God? What would be the most strategic choice as an investment of my life? How much _____ will it take? Is there a need? Is there a way? Are there enough people, finances, materials? What would prepare and develop me in the future? What are my motives? Is it to gain approval or acceptance from someone, money, power or to stay comfortable?

3 Warnings in Discerning God's Will

Be careful of authoritative reliance on subjective means:

1. Be cautious of "the open door policy". This is saying that God's will is whatever opportunity works out for you. When Moses was leading the Israelites out of Egypt and ran into the Red Sea, which very well could have looked like a "closed door". Or when Paul and Silas were in jail and an earthquake opened the jail doors but they stayed put. Because they didn't interpret the literal "open door" as God wanting them to go through it, the jailer and his household came to put their faith in Christ. (Acts 16:22-40)

Sometimes a "closed door" may just be an opportunity to give God more glory. Just because an opportunity comes up, doesn't mean it is the best option for your time and resources.

2. Be careful to not judge God's will by your "feelings of peace". This is not scriptural *(and when it says God will give us peace that passes understanding it is not talking about decision making but worry).* If our feelings were the authority of God's will, Jesus would not have died on the cross. (Lk 22:42-44, Heb. 12:1-4) God can use our feelings and often times our desires can be in line with His desire, but when making decisions, it is unwise to use them alone since Jeremiah 17:9 tells us our heart is deceitful above all things.

Another example is in Acts 21:10-14, 20:22-23 when the Christians let their feelings try to govern Paul's decision, but Paul would not let the fear of hard times change his decision.

Faith is established on truth, and truth is not relative but established on fact, not hunches, feelings, impressions, looking for signs, or mystical experiences.

3. Be cautious of listening to ungodly counsel. **Everyone has an opinion and most people will share it with you. But just because someone is a good friend does not mean the advice they are giving you is godly. Before taking someone's advice make sure to weigh what they are saying against Scripture. Does what they are saying match up with God's Word or contradict? It might even be best to not talk about important decisions with friends who will encourage you to do the wrong thing.**

And finally, step out in faith. Faith is not waiting until you know 100%. Genuine faith is moving in that direction, putting confidence more in God's ability to guide or re-direct than in your ability to decide. It means putting your trust ultimately in God and not in self, circumstances, feelings or others.

The more we grow as Christians the more decisions we will make by faith in God, from seemingly big ones like who you'll marry, to seemingly small ones like what to watch on TV. It is important to be ready to trust God in your decision whether it turns out the way you expected or not. And remember that with God the process is as important as the product.

Setting Goals
Chapter Nine

I have a lot of fears in setting goals. Maybe you do to. In thinking about long term goals I wonder, *"How in the world am I suppose to know what is going to be and not be in 10 years? Who knows if I'll even be alive or if some tragedy happens and my dreams wont even be a possibility." "And what if I fail? And what if Jesus comes back before then? And will I even be healthy enough to do what I dream to do?"* And then on top of my own fears I hear from others, *"we need to live in the present."* And a host of other things.

But something in me wants to fight past the fear and confusion. To do the hard thing and not give in to the easy. Something deep down wants to cling to Jesus and understand and see how He does. And even more than the fear and confusion, a big part of me wants to be pleasing to the Lord, to be a good steward. So every so often I need to lift my eyes to the end, to the big picture so I don't drown in the now. That's why I make goals. It's easier not to and I might fail, but I want to be faithful to steward what the Lord has given me rather than be controlled by the tyranny of the urgent which doesn't result in great return.

But, not all planning and goal setting is beneficial. Just making goals without the end in mind is like my kids' little gerbils running on their wheel; activity void of real reward.

Setting goals requires wisdom. It takes seeing the big picture and then breaking it down to bite size pieces. So here's how I do it. I have a when I'm 55 years old goal. I write down all the things that needs to happen for my dream of what I would like my merged circles to look like when I'm 55. Then I work backward. I ask myself, *"In order for each of those strategic things that have to happen, what needs to happen for those to happen when I am 45?"* (I picked 55 because that is when all my kids will be 18.) Then I broke those down to when I'm 40 and then in the next year. And then ultimately into semesters (since I'm part of a college ministry, I think in terms of semesters. For other people maybe quarters would be better.) And then for making semester goals I use the SMART acronym. (Specific, Measurable, Attainable, Relevant and Time-bound/Trackable).

Long term goals are purposeful and life-giving because they enable me to see outside the right here and now of diapers, discipline and unloading the dishwasher twice a day. It helps me value now for I can see part of the purpose. I can see this season as a season of preparation. I am learning patience, communication, wisdom, self-control, servant-hood and so much more, things I will desperately need for then. Long term goals help me worship God in this season. They help me give my best now knowing it has an important purpose. So I make personal goals to help me glorify God the best I know how.

Harvard followed a graduating class for twenty five years to see what impact a written purpose statement would have on an individual's accomplishments. Only 3% of that class had written out their life goals and purposes. At the end of twenty five years the 3% who had written out goals had more net worth than the other 97% combined. John F. Kennedy was one of the 3% who had a written out purpose. He was killed before the twenty five years were finished but the main goal of his written purpose statement was to become President of the United States of America.

So the fear of not knowing what life will be like in 10 years doesn't need to be a fear. God knows, and maybe He will let you partner with Him in setting goals to be there, maybe not. But even if you die with goals still in hand, you will be found a faithful steward. Because really success in the eyes of God is being faithful and obedient to take initiative in the power of the Holy Spirit and leave the results up to God.

Set Goals

Do a throne check and then take some time to look back at what you wrote for how to merge your mission, current reality and uniqueness for God's glory. Using this, think about what you want to be true of you and your life ten years from now. Then break it down into five years from now and a year from now. For the things you'd like to be true of you and your life in a year come up with some SMART goals. (Specific, Measurable, Attainable, Relevant and Trackable).

Remember to not hold yourself to the standard of perfection, there will always be room to tweak and adjust your goals.

Staying Focused
Chapter Ten

"You will never know what a distraction is until you know what your goal and purpose are. You must enunciate what your final goal is. It is imperative that somehow, before God, you take that time to write out on a blank sheet of paper why you exist. How wonderful it would be to clearly write out what the purpose of your life is really about and in light of that determine what will refresh and rejuvenate you as you pursue that purpose." Ravi Zacharias

Tyranny of the urgent (doing whatever comes up because it's urgent) robs our family and ministry of effectiveness and efficiency. That's why it's so important to have Christ on the throne and clearly know your calling and long term goals broken down into short term goals. (Things we are supposed to steward, our behavior and gifts, not things we can't control like other people's decisions). Then we are able to make decisions not based on impulse but by faith of what the Lord has called us to. Then we are able to say no to good things because though something may seem good, it is actually squishing out the best. Our calling and goals help us discern the good from best.

The big rocks first illustration by Dr. Steven Covey helps make clear what happens when we are controlled by tyranny of the urgent rather than living by our calling and goals. The illustration starts with an empty jar and three different size rocks and sand. If you put the rocks and sand in at random you cannot fit all the rocks and sand. However if you put in the biggest rocks followed by the medium rocks, small rocks and then the sand, then it all fits in the jar. The biggest rocks in our life are our top priorities whereas the sand can be compared to the urgent, non-important things in our life that pull for our attention. To stay focused on the calling God has for us, we need the Lord to give us wisdom to discern the best from the good and the ability to say no to the things that don't fit into what He has called us to.

Personal Reflection

Evaluate your activities in light of your calling and determine whether those activities are distracting you from your calling or helping to accomplish it. What changes need to be made?

Look back through the workbook and spend some time praying and/or journaling your thoughts and feelings to the Lord.

Write down your calling, goals and action steps.

Other books by Laura

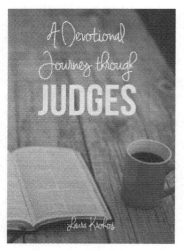

Judges is full of people with struggles and insecurities just like you and I. But not only can we relate to the people's stories in Judges but we can draw insightful and helpful principles that relate to us today and give us incredible glimpses of God's heart and character.

Judges has been compared to a Old Testament mirror of the church today. We can learn a lot from seeing how the the Lord interacted and dealt with His people in a society much like ours. But not only is Judges a relate-able book for today, it's full of stories making it incredibly engaging.

Beholding Him, Becoming Missional: Awakening to the Mission through the Study of First Samuel offers women the opportunity to behold the King and be transformed into living uniquely purposeful and missional lives. By the end of the study, women will walk away with minds and hearts that have been transformed through an intimate relationship with the King, and lives uniquely reflecting the King's heart and mission for the world.

All of Laura's books can be found at MissionalWomen.com and amazon.

64336797R00038

Made in the USA
Middletown, DE
11 February 2018